Getting a Squirrel to Focus Engage and Persuade Today's Listeners

Going Nuts for Getting a Squirrel to Focus

As Founder and President of Legacy MedSearch, a retained medical device recruitment firm, I know that the only way to be successful in business is to hone your communication skills. The ability to get our persuasive message across has led to earning the title of "one of North America's Most Influential Recruiters." Now the skills needed to get that persuasive message across are all in one place. This is a must read for Senior Executives wanting to communicate with their stakeholders, managers wishing to motivate their employees, salespeople looking to increase closing rates and jobseekers who want to enhance their candidacy during the interview. Simply put, Dr. Scott breaks down the communication process into simple, actionable steps. Companies who use the ACORN Communication Strategy™ *will likely see both improvement in internal communication and a growth in their revenue since sales and marketing teams will have a firm grasp on the customers' needs and motivations and be better equipped to target their message to close business.*

Paula Rutledge
Founder and President, Legacy MedSearch

Finally, a book that speaks to the small business entrepreneur! I've read many books that claim to offer solutions to small business owners but this book is the first that spoke to me. Dr. Scott's ACORN Communication Strategy™ changed my approach to how I market and promote my small business. Not only is this book clear, concise and easy to understand, but it's also easy to execute. I was able to effectively communicate my message to my potential clients. The response I've gotten from them has been overwhelming. Before I even finished the book, I was off and running; I was motivated! Implementing this unique and efficient ACORN Communication Strategy™ really made a big difference with little effort. This no-nonsense book gave me practical solutions and made a big impact on my small business!

Kelly McBride
Founder, Belly Pilates

While you may never use ACORN to get a real squirrel to focus, you will without a doubt become a more effective communicator with those that matter to you after reading this book. Dr. Scott's clever and practical approach to honing your message lays out clear, easy to understand principles that are useful in any profession. Getting a Squirrel to Focus *should be on the reading list of any results-oriented professional interested in becoming a more powerful, meaningful and persuasive communicator.*

Susan Little
Founder, Little Instructional Design

In Getting a Squirrel to Focus, *Dr. Patricia Scott has created a powerful ACORN of tested communication strategies, whatever the topic or the communication method. She models her message in this insightful little book with BIG IDEAS that gain attention, establish relevance, build affiliation and then effectively call listeners (and her readers) to action. Dr. Scott's career has spanned academia, corporations, nonprofits, and small entrepreneurial businesses. She knows how to make communication work to support every endeavor—from multi-million dollar campaigns to the everyday sales call. And she does so with a creativity that can even get a squirrel to focus. In this book, this trainer will train you for comparable results.*

Christina M. Genest
Associate Director
CCI – Corporate Communication International
at Baruch College/CUNY

Using real-life examples this book provides the tools necessary to get your message across. I was able to employ these concepts at work as well as in my personal life to make more persuasive arguments. Not only will your message be that much easier for your audience to understand, you will most likely get your way!

Heidi Hausner
Manager, Regulatory and Clinical Projects
Synthes, Inc.

Getting a Squirrel to Focus

Engage and Persuade Today's Listeners

Patricia B. Scott, Ph.D.

©2010 by Uhmms Publishing

Media, Pennsylvania 19063

Uhmms offers excellent discounts on this book when ordered in quantity for bulk purchase or special sales. For more information, please contact Uhmms Publishing.

www.uhmms.com
improve@uhmms.com

Company and product names mentioned herein are the trademarks or registered trademarks of their respective owners.

Printed in the United States of America

First printing: June, 2010

ISBN-10: 0-61-536858-1
ISBN-13: 978-0-61-536858-0

To the two acorns in my life: my beautiful daughter Emily and my husband Dan. They keep me focused on what is truly important, fulfill all my needs and sustain me with their constant and unconditional love.

Without their support and encouragement, this book would not have been possible.

Table of Contents

About the author

Dr. Scott had nearly fifteen years of corporate training experience while working in the medical device industry before becoming the founder of Uhmms. Uhmms is a communication consulting firm specializing in teaching you how to speak, lead and inspire.

Through keynote addresses, workshops, seminars, and on-line coaching, she provides a communication strategy so that your message can be heard loud and clear, despite all the noise around us. Uhmms standard course offerings include presentation skills, teaching technical information and elements of persuasion. Satisfied clients include Synthes, Johnson and Johnson, Pilling-Weck, Stryker, AO North America, Vertebron, Medartis and Genentech.

For the past seven years Dr. Scott has been a lecturer in the Communication Program at the Wharton School of the University of Pennsylvania. She has also lectured extensively for the Wharton MBA for Executives Program and the Wharton Executive Education Program at the Aresty Institute for Executive Education.

Dr. Scott has been invited to address the Conference on Corporate Communication in Wroxton, England, three times. The conference is offered in association with Corporate Communication International at Baruch College, City University of New York. At her first conference, she was awarded "Best Paper of Conference" for her analysis of social, task and semantic networks of knowledge workers. Her work has been published in *Corporate Communications: An International Journal*, a peer-reviewed journal Published by Emerald Publications. She has been asked to continue to serve annually on the program committee for the Conference on Corporate Communication.

In 2008 Dr. Scott was awarded an advisory board position for the Master of Arts program in Corporate Communication at Baruch College of the City University of New York.

Education

Rutgers University, New Brunswick, NJ—Ph.D. (Corporate Communication)

Farleigh Dickinson University, Madison, NJ—M.A. (Corporate and Organizational Communication)

University of Dayton, Dayton, OH—B.A. (Communication, Secondary Education)

Foreword

We all know them and probably work with a few—the busy multitasking professionals with one hand on a Blackberry and another on the computer keyboard. Too many distractions and shorter attention spans all conspire to make effective communication to these professionals difficult to achieve. More now than ever before, communicators struggle to break through the noise and communicate persuasively. Then, along comes *Getting a Squirrel to Focus*, a concise book that includes just the right mix of theory and practical tips to make it a must-have on the desk of any busy professional who wants to be a more persuasive communicator.

Rather than decry the short attention spans of business audiences, Dr. Pat Scott takes this reality and turns it to a speaker's advantage—a handy trick given the complexity and volume of business information flowing through the workplace. The secret is, of course, to understand the audience, but that is more easily said than done. As a communication expert, Pat helps us understand how to get business audiences to focus on our message by laying out an easy-to-follow rubric she calls the ACORN Communication Strategy™. The kind of communication Pat advocates is a two-way, conversational and authentic exchange that seems like common sense, but is actually the result of a strategic approach to crafting and delivering persuasive messages. She'll help you to find common ground with even the toughest audiences, and help you communicate in a way that achieves clarity and understanding.

We've worked with Pat Scott for many years, and her expertise and enthusiasm for teaching communication skills is remarkable. As you read *Getting a Squirrel to Focus* we're sure you'll recognize her gifts for making an often intimidating subject accessible and fun.

Margaret Lambires
Carl Maugeri

Senior Associate Directors
The Wharton Communication Program
University of Pennsylvania

Introduction

Getting your message across is harder today than it has ever been.

More information, more distractions and shorter attention spans provide competition for every message you create.

More information, more distractions and shorter attention spans provide competition for every message you create. It is hard for us to listen, and we jump from one thought to the next very quickly. This jumpy and sporadic listening behavior reminds me of the squirrels I see in my yard. They are constantly moving and seem fidgety and unfocused. The only thing that seems to gain and hold their interest is an acorn.

Through my years of experience in research and teaching I have found that squirrels are like today's audience. There is a way to get their attention and keep it. The ACORN Communication Strategy™ presented in this book is an efficient communication tool to get your audience focused on your message. Remember: no matter how brilliant you are, if you can't get your message across, you can't lead, sell, educate, persuade, advocate or help.

But are today's listeners' attention spans really similar to squirrels'?

Fact about squirrels' attention spans:

- One-second attention span on normal things, but can focus for about four minutes on an acorn.[1]

Facts about humans' attention spans:

- When browsing the web, our attention span can be the same as a goldfish's—9 seconds.[2]

- In recent years, the op-ed has been shortened by 25%, "no doubt a concession to generations raised on new media.... Especially in this age of shortened attention spans, readers are more apt to abandon you mid-article than to follow you to a second issue."[3]

- 99% of business people said their attention spans are shorter today than three years ago.[4]

Today's audience—Human squirrels

There is more data out there today than there has ever been before. The world population is on track to produce about 988 billion gigabytes of data per year by 2010 and the amount of information that is being produced is *expanding exponentially*.[5] Unfortunately, attention spans have not expanded exponentially to meet the new quantities of data. Attention spans have changed over time.

Attention spans have changed over time.

In the 1800's the Lincoln-Douglas debates were read from paper to their audiences.[6] In October of 1854 Douglas delivered a three-hour address. Lincoln followed with a three-hour rebuttal. Douglas returned with a one-hour rebuttal of his own. Obviously, he spoke without pictures or images (or PowerPoint).

What kind of American audience today would listen to seven hours of oratory debate, especially considering these gentlemen were not even presidential candidates?

Today, American audiences are reluctant to even hear a Presidential State of the Union Address. Now, even when the message is important, we often aren't good listeners.

When it was rumored that the State of the Union Address to be given by President Barack Obama might be scheduled to interfere with the final season premiere of a television show called *Lost*, fans of the show were in an uproar. The scheduling battle took center stage and was reported in the *Washington Post*. ABC radio reporter Ann Compton asked about the date conflict at a White House press briefing. Press Secretary Robert Gibbs responded, "I don't foresee a scenario in which millions of people who hope to finally get some conclusion with *Lost* are preempted by the president."[7]

It seems that now we would rather be entertained than informed. Your message is competing against short attention spans, information overload and other mindless distractions.

How can you get your message to be as special as an acorn is to a squirrel?

How can you get your message to be as special as an acorn is to a squirrel? Is there a way to not only be heard, but to be memorable and persuasive—to affect the listener?

As Erma Bombeck so aptly said in 1971, "It seemed rather incongruous that in a society of supersophisticated communication, we often suffer from a shortage of listeners."[8]

Take a minute and think about the squirrels in your life. Boss? Spouse? Children? Friends? Clients? Executives? Students?

Your ACORN

This book will provide an easy and practical way to change your message strategy to make it much more efficient and effective.

This book will provide an easy and practical way to change your message strategy to make it much more efficient and effective. It will help you create *your* acorn. When squirrels have an acorn they focus, and their attention span is increased by 23,900%. If you can create the equivalent of an acorn for your listeners, you have a greater chance to get your message across.

Through rigorous academic research and teaching hundreds of corporate managers, sales representatives and Master of Business Administration (MBA) students, I've found that there are five essential ingredients to make your message an acorn. The ingredients are:

Audience

Credibility

Order

Remember me

Need to connect

Audience – It is not about what you want to say, but what the listener can hear. What will they get out of the information you are providing? Remember that we have "remote control" length attention spans. If what you are saying does not interest us or is irrelevant to us, we will merely click you off and stop listening. If it is not an acorn for us, we simply move on to the next message.

Credibility – Why are *you* the one we should listen to for this information? In a society where virtually everyone has a voice and everyone has a forum to express his or her opinion, how do you distinguish yourself from the rest of the "noise"? What will compel us to believe that you are knowledgeable and that you are the one we should listen to?

Order of message – Through research we know that we can no longer build up suspense to get to our key point or main message. Unless it is a great story in a casual setting, we would rather just get to the point. Especially in the business setting or in sales, we need to rethink the structure of our messages so that the listener will give us a chance to get our point across.

Remember me – Since we are a society of poor listeners, it is now the speaker's responsibility to help us understand the information easily. The listener should not have to work hard to understand what you are saying. We shouldn't force our listeners to take a sip of water from a fire hose. Even when you have a lot to say, the speaker needs to make the information digestible in easy-to-chew bites so that we can internalize it and remember it.

Need to connect – Gone are the days when we can claim that there is no place for emotional connection to the message in the business world. Research has shown that humans need to feel something to be moved to action. A logical series of facts may win the argument, but that is not enough when we want our audience to change a belief or move to a specific action. Tools such as word choice and visual language can help us connect without being too "soft" for serious conversations.

The need to persuade

At a seminar recently I was helping a group of senior executives simply do a better job from the podium. They were all competent speakers; they knew to stand up straight and look at us and vary their voices and use gestures. They were confident and easy to listen to, and yet, even with all those positive traits, it was a struggle to pay attention to them.

Their job was to present very technical information to a wide variety of audiences. These executives saw the importance of their job as relating this information. It didn't seem to matter much that the audience couldn't understand, didn't want to listen and had absolutely no interest in the information that the executives thought was so important.

As we progressed through the seminar, the presenters had to fundamentally change their thinking about what they were trying to accomplish. Each time they gave a message, it wasn't just a "data dump" but a missed opportunity for persuasion.

Every time you speak on a topic, you should be trying to persuade your audience.

Every time you speak on a topic, you should be trying to persuade your audience. Even if the topic is not controversial, you are trying to persuade the audience. You want them to agree with your point of view, or agree that you have done enough research to make you the expert, or to see your vision or solution going forward.

When these executives presented, even just reviewing company numbers and results, they had slide after slide of data with no unifying message, and nothing for the audience to do or feel anything about. There was simply no acorn to capture and sustain interest. They chose to inform rather than transform their audience.

To begin our process it is important to see each message as an opportunity to share meaning with your audience. Not just information, not just facts or stories, but meaning. Persuasion is more than simply "winning the argument." The word persuade is defined as "to move by argument, entreaty, or expostulation to a belief, position, or course of action."[9]

Through persuasion we do not want to win an argument; we want to move someone to a new belief or action. Creating an ACORN for your audience is an important tool in accomplishing this.

Is it worth spending just a few extra minutes to put an easy communication strategy together? Does it matter what you say first? Does it matter what order the structure of your talk is in? It is your responsibility as a speaker to make the information easy to hear, understandable and memorable.

Building the ACORN is not difficult because it is common sense. It doesn't take long to do. Yet, this easy strategy can have a transformational effect on your message and how your audience responds to it.

Each of the following chapters will talk about an ingredient needed to make your message an ACORN for your listeners. The final chapters will offer some concrete advice and tools on how to become a powerful speaker and leader by getting a message across to your listeners.

An aside:

My apologies to my colleagues in Australia, which is one of the very few places on earth that do not have squirrels. Squirrels are found in the Americas, Europe, Asia and Africa.

Interestingly, in the United States, the greatest concentration of squirrels is in Lafayette Park across from the White House.[10]

Chapter One: **A**udience

Relevance

Let me put this bluntly: basically, we really only care about ourselves and our own needs. I am not talking here about the needs of the speaker; I am referring only to the audience. When I am listening, the only thing that will get my attention and keep it is something I need or care about.

As Dale Carnegie said, "You can close more business in two months by becoming interested in other people than you can in two years by trying to get people interested in you."[11]

As listeners, we live in a "remote control" society. I do it and you probably do, too: turn on the TV, start clicking through channels, and keep clicking until you catch a piece of information that you need. It is our search for relevance. As we watch, we think, "No, we don't need the latest food processor right now, don't need new jewelry, don't need to know the scores of all the weekend football games, don't need to see that report on the disaster again, but oh, yes, I do need to know the weather." So we stop there until our need is fulfilled and then we move on.

It is the same for the squirrel and the acorn. The acorn represents the squirrel's need for survival. That need surpasses all else so the squirrel has the uncanny ability to focus on it for a long time.

Your brain and relevance

Scientists understand how this process of focusing works. There is a part of the hindbrain called the Reticular Activating System (RAS). This is the part of the brain that serves as a filter for our incoming messages. It decides what information is relevant. The relevant stuff becomes part of our stream of consciousness.

It also controls wakefulness and the ability to let ourselves fall asleep.

How does the RAS work and how does it decide what is relevant for us? Quite simply, there is a hierarchy to determine relevance. When information comes into the RAS, the thing it looks for first is need. Does this information fulfill a need? Is it relevant to me? If it is not, it gets filtered out.

As audiences listen, they are listening to see what is important, needed, and relevant to them.

As audiences listen, they are listening to see what is important, needed, and relevant to them. Even if the subject is the speaker's passion and the delivery is great, if I don't care about it, if it is not important or relevant to me specifically, I will not continue to listen. The words will just become background noise.

Imagine yourself in a crowded train station. Lots of noise, lots of commotion, lots of announcements being made over the loudspeaker. You are aware of all of the noise, but not necessarily paying close attention to it. Then, the next announcement includes your train number and name, and suddenly you try to block out all the noise and listen to this relevant piece of information. The RAS tells the rest of the body to get ready to respond more specifically to input. It then tells the rest of the central nervous system to search for more information and coordinate the data to know what to do next.

What is not needed or relevant becomes "noise." Keep in mind that what is "noise" to one person may be relevant to another. For example, each week I skim through the ads that come with my Sunday paper. Even if there is a killer sale on new refrigerators, I usually just throw the ad away. If I don't need a new refrigerator, no matter how good the deal is, I am just not interested.

However, if my old refrigerator just died, the ad that was trash just a week ago now becomes the focus of my search and probably the focus of all our family discussions that Sunday morning.

Therefore, you have to find what is relevant for your specific audience. Even if your overall key message is the same, the strategy with which you deliver it has to change with the audience.

What's In It For Me? WIIFM

As we craft our ACORN, how can we get the audience's RAS to focus and take in the information? **WIIFM.**

WIIFM is the key to the entire acorn.

WIIFM is the key to the entire acorn. WIIFM stands for "What's In It For Me."

As an audience member we need to hear and understand the WIIFM at the very beginning of the message.

At a seminar I taught recently for a group of middle managers of an organization, one of the exercises was for the participants to present a somewhat controversial topic and persuade me to their point of view. In this seminar I didn't limit the topics to business, but to any persuasive conversation they were going to have in the next couple of weeks. Most of the time the participants stick to business topics, but there was one gentleman in my class who wanted to see if the tools we were teaching through the ACORN Communication Strategy™ would translate to improving his everyday life.

What was his burning controversial and persuasive topic? He wanted to convince his wife that they needed a 60" plasma TV in their living room.

"Fine," I said, "pretend I am your wife, how will you start your request?" He thought for a moment and said, "Honey, you know how much I love to watch football…" I immediately made a buzzer sound and asked him to sit back down. He looked shocked. "My wife loves me," he said, "and she would want me to be happy."

While I am sure he has a great relationship with his wife, and while I am sure she wants him to be happy (maybe), there is nothing in it for *her*. The WIIFM of *his* statement was all about him—all about fulfilling *his* need.

This gentleman respectfully disagreed with me and decided to try that very approach on his wife that evening. When he came back to class the second day he told me about what happened. He did start with, "Honey, you know how much I love to watch football…" She immediately smiled and said, "I know," and then she followed up with, "but it is just too expensive for the sixteen Sundays of football season. I just don't think we should right now. We have other house priorities that need to come first."

I have often seen the same pattern in failed sales calls. The sales representative has a couple of years of experience, so he or she is technically competent and has been around long enough to finally get a chance to talk to a key decision maker. No one will set up a meeting for the sales representative to extol the virtues of their product for thirty minutes, so the sales representative has to catch the client when he or she can.

In these instances I often hear the sales person say, "Good morning, I just wanted to talk to you today so I could show you our new product." Then he or she starts the data dump. The client stops really listening after the sales person uses "I" twice in the first dozen words. Why should the client listen? What is in it for him or her? Even if eventually one of the product features would really help, it is too late, the client has stopped listening.

Remember, it is always about what's in it for them. Unless we can get the listener's RAS to see this information as something that is needed, it doesn't really matter what the rest of the message is because it will just be noise.

Don't think of what you want to accomplish with the message. What will your audience get from listening to you? It is not about what *you* want, but finding and solving the needs of the listener. As Dale Carnegie aptly said, "I like brownies, but I fish with worms."

To provide you the opportunity to practically apply what you find in this book, I would like you now to turn to the ACORN Communication Strategy™ Worksheet in Chapter Seven. Feel free to make copies of the worksheet to use as you go through the chapters of this book.

Using this worksheet as an exercise, I would like you to think about a persuasive conversation that you will need to have in the next couple of weeks, whether it is for business or personal reasons. Be as specific as you can. Think of your intended audience and try to stay away from generalities like "upper management" or "client." Use a specific example, like Lisa the head of human resources or Jim the purchaser at my target client's office.

Now, think about how well you know this person or group. What do you know about him, her or them? As you can see, if you don't know them well, the WIIFM is much harder to find. If you are tempted to think that you will just use the biggest benefit of your product or best piece of evidence regardless of the audience, you will only end up persuading those who by luck need what you are selling. Instead, provide them what they need.

Keep in mind that knowing your audience is far more than just knowing the demographics of the audience. While it may be somewhat helpful to know the age range, gender mix, tenure, education level, etc., those pieces of information generally do not lead to a really strong WIIFM.

Ask open-ended questions to find out:

What drives them?

What do they like?

What do they need?

What will solve their problem/frustrations/fears?

What goals do you have in common?

When constructing the WIIFM keep in mind that the more homogenous the audience, the easier it is to construct a WIIFM. You can create a very specific WIIFM customized for that person or specific group of people.

The more diverse the audience, the broader the WIIFM will be.

We see this every day on the news. What would appeal to a large and somewhat diverse audience? How will you stop them from changing the channel during the commercial? A really broad WIIFM is, "Five things you must know before your next visit to the grocery store." The majority of the audience goes to the store or knows someone who does, so that very broad WIIFM may keep their interest and at least get them to begin listening.

Keep in mind that communication happens in a moment-by-moment way. The way we hear, understand and make sense of language happens as we listen to the individual words. For example, I might say, "Last night, I broke my toe...nail...clipper." As the sentence progresses, the meaning and feeling associated with the idea change.

With the WIIFM, the goal is just to get your audience to start listening.

With the WIIFM, the goal is just to get your audience to start listening. That's it. Just having the squirrel recognize and get excited about spotting an acorn has to be the first step. No matter how good the acorn tastes and how nutritious it is for him, none of it matters if he never saw the acorn to begin with.

▸ Application

Now it's your turn. Here are the pieces of information you need to complete first to start your message. Please feel free to use the worksheet from Chapter Seven to begin your practice.

Specific situation:

Audience

WIIFM

The TV guy I mentioned earlier had to re-examine his plan to sell his wife on the idea of a new 60" plasma TV. This time he thought about his wife, what she likes, what problems the TV could solve and what she really cares about.

It turns out that she loves to entertain. While she was growing up her mother and father often had parties and get-togethers. When she was young, she loved these gatherings and often spoke of them with fondness to her husband. She told stories of getting dressed up for one of their grand parties and helping her mother make snacks for the more informal celebrations.

The husband decided this time to make his WIIFM about his wife. This time he said, "Honey, I know how much you used to love it when your parents hosted parties and entertained their friends. You know, maybe we should really start to do more of that. Now that the holidays are over, why don't we plan a fun party for the Super Bowl or St. Patrick's Day? We can decorate the house, finally get a nice new TV and share some special time with our friends and family."

This time, the WIIFM was directed toward the wife's interests and she was at least listening. She might not yet be persuaded, but she was listening. He let her see the acorn.

Chapter Two: Credibility

Now that you have your listener's attention by keeping the Audience (the **A** of ACORN) in mind and targeting his or her WIIFM (What's In It For Me), how do you keep it?

In Chapter One, we discussed how communication is a moment-by-moment science. It is true that if you don't get someone's attention and the topic is not relevant, the rest of what you say may not count for much. It is also true that once you have their attention, the next thing you say can make or break the rest of your argument. How do you get a few more minutes of their attention? How can you start with relevance and end in persuasion? What is the next step?

Credibility. Now that you have my attention, why are you the right person to listen to on this topic? How can you convince me that it is worth listening to you instead of seeking other sources of information on this topic? Are you worth my time?

Credibility has long been known as one of the foundations of persuasion. How long? Since around 367 B.C. In that year Aristotle went to Athens to become a student in Plato's Academy because at an early age he had a sincere interest in philosophy. He liked, respected and learned much from Plato, but he ultimately rejected much of Plato's work because Aristotle was far more pragmatic than the fundamentals of Platonic concepts would allow.

Plato wanted to determine how to achieve happiness in secular society and to learn to what extent rational control of emotions could play a part in that happiness. Aristotle was interested in logic, rhetoric and political theory, and he based his ethics on those concepts rather than on religious beliefs, the afterlife or transcendent ideas.

In 350 B.C. Aristotle offered courses in rhetoric. These courses are thought to have been open to the public and were combined with practical exercises in speaking. He believed that persuasion has three essential components:

Ethos – character or credibility

Pathos – emotion

Logos – logical argument[12]

We will discuss all three of these components throughout the course of this book, but for now we will focus on ethos.

It is generally believed that there are three keys to ethos: competence, trustworthiness and expertise.[13] Through my experience with corporate clients and Wharton MBA students, I have found that things might be even simpler.

Now that the world is changing and our communication time is shortened, it seems that you can have either personal credibility or credentialed credibility.

Now that the world is changing and our communication time is shortened, it seems that you can have either personal credibility or credentialed credibility.

Personal credibility

Personal credibility is present when a relationship already exists with your listener. This type of credibility is often made up of elements like competence and trustworthiness (trustworthiness is sometimes also described as sincerity, honesty, genuineness, confidence or having personal integrity) that must be continually demonstrated over time or come from a known and accepted reputation.

In work settings competence is often seen as a credibility builder. Your ability to do a task or handle a situation consistently with proven results will develop your reputation and personal credibility. Experience with you and your service or product is the best way to show competence and then gain reputation to affect your credibility. Again, the key here is that competence is built over time, but can then be leveraged once you are within a network of believers.

Trustworthiness is perceived when someone is consistently honest or truthful and these characteristics are demonstrated again and again over time. Trustworthiness is also viewed as consistent sincerity.

Sincere is derived from Latin and literally means "without wax" (*sine*—without, and *cera*—wax) and has an interesting etymology. Folk etymology has two possible explanations for the history of the word. In the first explanation, the Romans demanded tributes from the Greeks so the Greeks made and presented "marble" statues. These statues were actually made from wax and quickly melted in the sun. Therefore a sincere statue would have been one made without wax and would have been an honest tribute.

In the second explanation, dishonest sculptors in Rome or Greece would cover any flaws in their works with wax to deceive the viewer. So in this case, a sincere sculpture would mean that its perfection was honest.[14]

As difficult as personal credibility (competence and trustworthiness) is to gain due to its need to be continually proven and improved, it is very easy to lose. Credibility is gained in drips and lost in gallons. So there is a need for consistent authenticity. There needs to be a proven and continual consistency not just in your actions, but also between what you say and what you do.

The year 2009 was marked by one of the worst financial crises in recent history. Many businesses, banks and insurance companies were failing due to the losses in the stock market and the failing economy. The government wanted to help stabilize institutions whose failure could damage many other businesses as well as harm individual investors. The government also wanted to take action in order to help retain consumer confidence. To do this, they "bailed out" some large institutions.

In one example, in September 2009, the United States Federal Reserve extended an $85 billion emergency loan to American International Group (AIG). Less than one week after receiving the government bailout (consisting of taxpayers' money), AIG spent nearly half a million dollars on a corporate retreat at the St. Regis Monarch Beach Resort in Dana Point, California. Taxpayers were outraged that this lavish eight-day retreat racked up nearly $24,000 on spa treatments, nearly $7,000 on golf and almost $150,000 on banquets.[15]

In AIG's defense, they booked the meeting months before the initial loan from the federal government. This type of trip was also a standard practice in the industry. Face-to-face meetings and these incentive trips rewarding top producing self-employed agents have shown to have a positive return on investment for the company.

But as a Bloomberg article quoted one business professor, "Whether the company's behavior is wrong on an absolute basis doesn't really matter. It's become a question of perception and it seems that they're being viewed as behaving unethically."[16]

AIG's credibility was seriously damaged from this one act. The company worked for 90 years to build its reputation, trustworthiness and competence. Their performance made them the world's largest insurance company, with employees in 130 different countries. With just one act they showed us inconsistency between what they said and what they did, and the public and media could scarcely get their fill of news and criticism.

Credentialed credibility

Credentialed credibility is most important when personal credibility has not yet been established, or is on shaky ground.

Credentialed credibility is quite simply expertise.

Credentialed credibility is quite simply expertise. To have credentialed credibility, you must either have a specialized area of knowledge or have done enough research or investigation to use others' credentialed credibility to your advantage.

For example, if you have specialized knowledge from an advanced degree, licenses, years of experience or even access to a unique experience, you may be seen as having credentialed credibility. This makes sense. We put more stock in advice or opinions from an expert than a non-expert. Would you rather get automotive advice from an experienced, licensed mechanic or from your plumber?

If you do not have first-hand experience or knowledge, you may also gain some credentialed credibility by using sources that already have credentialed credibility. Which statement would you be more likely to believe?

"It seems like it is easier for people to find jobs today than last year."

or

"According to a report in the *New York Times*, unemployment is down compared to this same time last year."

Letting the credibility of the *New York Times* rub off on you is a good way to gain credentialed credibility. The obvious caveat with this is that the source you use also needs to be trusted and have credentialed credibility. For example, if the basis for your logic is an article you read in *National Enquirer* or *Star* magazine (those, in my opinion, with shaky reputations and inaccurate reporting), your credibility will not be enhanced.

Whether it is personal or credentialed, credibility is important to your effectiveness as a communicator.

Sandy Allgeier, author of an article in *Training and Development*, said it well:

> Simply put, if you have no credibility, people won't trust you. If people do not trust you, you won't persuade them. And if you can't persuade, you will never be able to problem solve, innovate, or lead. In an ideas economy, you will become increasingly irrelevant.[17]

Credibility has been important for over 2,300 years, since Aristotle taught the importance of ethos. But today we face even more daunting challenges because in our "squirrel" society we have two more obstacles to overcome: competition and ignorance.

What happens to credibility in today's society when everyone can have a voice? There is fierce competition to be heard, to be believed and to distinguish ourselves through our, in some cases, self-proclaimed expertise. It has become more important than ever to let your earned credibility show and to distinguish yourself.

With all this competition and the tenuous nature of credibility, can credibility be sustained? Because of the many competing voices, people are more skeptical of what they hear and are increasingly wary of bias, opinion and dishonesty.

In September 2009 a Pew Research Survey found that the majority of respondents felt that news reports are inaccurate and that news programs are politically biased. These numbers reveal that the credibility of the news media has hit a two-decade low.[18]

So what is the role of credibility becoming? Because we face an explosion of information and an ever-increasing number of online information sources, it has been suggested that the role of credibility has changed. Now, credibility can only be used to separate the good from the bad, and not used to gain confidence.[19]

For most people, just the distinction between good and bad will never be enough. Even though everyone can now have a voice, most of us understand the importance of taking credibility into account before we are persuaded.

This brings us to the other obstacle we face, which is credibility ignorance. As noted before, the use of authentic credibility can give us a necessary boost toward persuasion as long as the listener accepts you as having personal or credentialed credibility. Or, at the very least, it can help us determine shades of difference between competing claims.

Fewer than 50% of high-school seniors can tell if a website was objective or from a biased source.[20] This is an alarming statistic. What will happen if credibility ignorance becomes commonplace?

If we cannot sustain our individual credibility, protect it, and demonstrate it, our ability to persuade and be heard will be greatly diminished.

If we cannot sustain our individual credibility, protect it, and demonstrate it, our ability to persuade and be heard will be greatly diminished. We need to use credibility as a powerful persuasion tool to distinguish us and keep our audience engaged. If we cannot do that, we don't have much hope of getting our messages across.

Jay Conger, a well-regarded authority on persuasion, said:

> ...it is important to note that credibility along
> either line can be built [personal credibility]
> or bought [credentialed credibility]. Indeed,
> it must be, or the next steps are an exercise in
> futility.[21]

▸ Application

*Remember the TV guy from the last chapter? When last
we heard him, he found his wife's WIIFM—gaining
the ability to entertain and have parties in their home.
Now he needs to convince her not only of the TV he
wants, but also that he knows the right TV to buy.*

*He can use either kind of credibility to help get his point
across. If he has made good choices in the past (shown
competence in picking appropriate items) he can use his
personal credibility. We will assume he is already seen as
trustworthy and sincere.*

Or, he can use credentialed credibility. He could say something like, "To make sure we get the best quality TV for the best value while staying in our budget, I have done lots of research. I started out by going to Consumer Reports *to find the best objectively rated brand, looked at online reviews to see what others like us think of their quality and value, and then looked at all of the Sunday circulars to find the best price."*

Ultimately, he used source credibility to enhance his own credibility and continue on the road to persuasion.

Now it's your turn again. For your specific situation, audience and WIIFM, how will you weave in your credibility? Do you have both credentialed and personal credibility? How will you introduce it into the conversation?

Feel free to go to your worksheet and fill in how you will talk about your credibility.

Although credibility should always be present, it does not always need to be explicitly expressed.

Although credibility should always be present, it does not always need to be explicitly expressed. If your credibility is already well known for this particular audience, and for this particular topic, you do not need to spend much (or any) time verbalizing it. For example, if President Barack Obama makes an address about government policy, he usually does not spend any time introducing himself as the president, or recalling his experience or service. It is already known and understood.

Be careful, though. Being credible in one area does not make you universally credible. I was coaching some sales representatives on how to better present their product in a short time span. They were introducing a new product. Even though they had established personal credibility with a customer they had known for a while, they were not yet seen as "expert" on this new product. They had personal credibility but needed credentialed credibility as well to close the sale.

Chapter Three: **O**rder of message

Presumably you are a subject matter expert in something. If you weren't, you probably would not have the opportunity to speak or need to persuade very often. In the last two chapters we talked about how to show your squirrel not just that you have an acorn, but that the acorn is good and worth eating and will fulfill the squirrel's need.

We have seen the importance of relating to the needs of the **A**udience, as well as the importance of displaying your **C**redibility in fulfilling those needs (the **A** and **C** of our ACORN Communication Strategy™).

But, of course, you have much more to say. You have facts, evidence, anecdotes, experiences, sources, proof, and details to get across. In this chapter we will focus on the body of your message and, most importantly, the **O**rder that the body of the message should be in.

Perhaps this is a good way to think of the importance of message order: Our squirrel is holding an acorn in his two eager little hands, and he looks around to make sure that eating is currently his biggest need (not the need for shelter from a hawk!). He examines it, makes sure it is good, and is now ready to take his first bite. What part should he eat first to get the most health benefit? What if he can only take one bite before he sees a hawk coming? Does it matter? Does what you say first and the order of you message matter? Is it all the same as long as you get all your information out?

Information is not all weighted the same for the listener. An individual's judgment and decision making is greatly influenced by the way information is positioned. Message framing and presentation order affects the listener's cognitive processes.[22]

Framing

Framing a message is a way to help your listeners determine the meaning of a subject and help them choose one particular meaning over another.[23] How do we want the audience to see this message? What should their perspective be? Through what lens should they examine the material?

Framing is a necessary step in communication. When we choose a frame for our audience to help them interpret our message, it is not to confuse or manipulate. There is always a frame present. The speaker always has a frame and the listener always has a frame. The frame is based on past experience, relevance, prior knowledge, etc.

When we share our frame with our audience, we are attempting to share a common vision of the message. Do we want them to see the glass half empty or half full? When we introduce a topic, do we say, "Interestingly, these facts are true," or "Sadly, these facts are true," or "Surprisingly, these facts are true?" How we frame the facts will help the listener interpret them correctly.

The best explanation of a frame I have come across was this analogy:

> Suppose you and a colleague wagered on who could complete the same jigsaw puzzle first. A third party buys two copies of the same 350-piece puzzle, dumping the contents of both boxes on a table in front of each of you. Your opponent has access to the box with a picture of the completed puzzle. You do not. Who will win?

> A frame is to a persuasive argument as the picture of a completed puzzle is to the jumbled pieces of the puzzle. Both show the "big picture" and provide implicit rules for putting the pieces together. Without the picture and without the frame, chaos prevails over coherence.[24]

How the frame is constructed will help the audience clearly understand the key message or main point that you are trying to communicate. As the analogy indicates, the frame must be clearly defined early in the message. It would not be helpful to see the box cover after the puzzle is complete.

Presentation order

As mentioned earlier, in addition to the frame, the order of your message also has an effect on the listener. There are two main ways that you can create your message. You can either have your key message first, or have your key message last. These structures are sometimes referred to as a persuasive or narrative structure respectively.

In the persuasive structure your key message, along with its frame, comes first. The key message is followed by the evidence, logic, argument or data. This structure can be represented by a simple triangle.

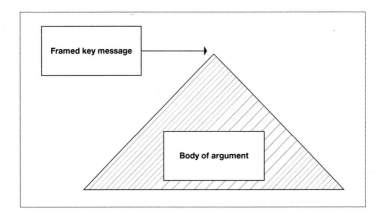

In the narrative structure the triangle is inverted. In this approach you first provide the argument and detail, and then conclude with the frame and the key message. This structure is how we have been sharing information for centuries. It is the structure of stories and jokes. In this structure, the punch line is at the end. The audience is teased along, and then there is the big reveal. Diagrammatically, it looks like this.

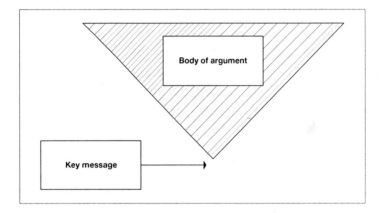

Of these two types of structure, is there one that is more effective for persuasion? Although the name already has given it away, the persuasive structure is the more effective presentation order.

When the message has a high degree of relevance, putting the most important or key message first has the greatest impact on the listener.

When the message has a high degree of relevance, putting the most important or key message first has the greatest impact on the listener. (We will make an assumption here that the message you are trying to create for your listeners will be made relevant for them through the use of your WIIFM from Chapter One. Refer to Chapter One for the importance of relevance for your audience.)

Conversely, for messages of low, personal or casual relevance (like a joke or story about your friend's weekend), the effect on the listener is better when the key message or main point comes at the end of the message. Once again, it is all about relevance.[25]

For example, consider this analogy. I am at the store picking up some groceries for dinner and as I drive down the street to my house, I notice that fire trucks surround the house. I realize my house may be on fire, which frightens me because I know that my family is home. I get out of the car quickly and run to the fire chief. He sees the question in my eyes and begins to tell me the story.

Apparently, my kids were hungry, so instead of waiting for me, at approximately 5:32pm my husband began to cook them grilled cheese sandwiches. During the cooking process, he got distracted; some cheese began to burn, starting a fire, setting all the smoke detectors off and summoning the fire department. Luckily, by the time the fire trucks arrived, the fire was out, and everyone was safe. No real damage was done.

That is a narrative way to tell the story. And if you are a mere passerby, with only curiosity, that is a fine way to tell the details of the story. But, if you are me, for whom the outcome of the story is most relevant, the last two sentences are the ones I really care about.

For a highly relevant message, the persuasive structure—beginning, "The fire is out, everyone is safe, and there is no real damage"—would have had a greater effect on how I heard the message. Since my need (relevance) was not fulfilled, and I didn't know whether the story had a positive or negative end (frame), I would have a hard time paying attention to the details and facts of the story. I first want the message to fulfill my need and show me how to interpret the facts, and then to provide detail and evidence.

The persuasive structure not only makes some intuitive sense, it has been proven to be true. In 1994, Haugtvedt and Wegener conducted a study involving 137 students. The goal of the study was to determine what factors determine the effectiveness of presentation order.

The students were broken into four groups. Two of the groups were considered high relevance and two groups were considered low relevance. The high relevance groups were informed that recently released Federal Energy Program documents suggested that nuclear power plants were going to be built in their own and several nearby states.

The low relevance groups were informed that recently released Federal Energy Program documents suggested that nuclear power plants were going to be built in distant states.

Each group then received the same pro and con messages about the nuclear power plants. The pro and con messages were proven to be equally strong arguments.

One high relevance group heard the message in the pro/con order and the other group heard the message in the the con/pro order.

The high relevance students were more favorable to the pro message when it came first and less favorable to the pro message when it came last. They reacted to whichever message was given to them first (the persuasive structure).

The results were predictably opposite for the low relevance group. For them, they were more favorable to the pro message when it came last and less favorable to the pro message when it came first. They reacted to whichever message was given to them last (the narrative structure).

Those with high relevance responded to the message that was given using the persuasive structure. Those with low relevance responded to the message that was given using the narrative structure.[26]

The persuasive structure is the most effective way to communicate if we want to persuade. For this structure to work best for us, we first need to establish the WIIFM to make the Reticular Activating System see the message as relevant. This WIIFM must fulfill the need and provide the framed key message right in the beginning.

We see evidence of this every day if we watch television ads. Do you notice that for some ads you remember what company the ad was promoting, but for others, you remember the catchy ad, but have no idea what the commercial was for?

The point at which the ad tells you the brand name affects your memory of it and how it links to the specific product. Advertising is more effective if the advertised brand name is revealed at the beginning of the message and is much less effective if withheld until the end of the message.

Learning is a process of creating associations between pieces of information. The temporal order of the message plays a critical role facilitating the linkage of reactions from one piece of information to the next.

A study was conducted in which variations of the same advertisement were shown to 270 participants. The only difference between the variations was the placement of the brand name or logo either at the beginning, middle or end of the message.

The researchers found that there was a significant effect of brand-name placement on brand attitude. Putting the brand name at the beginning of the ad rather than waiting until the end enhanced the persuasive impact of the ad.[27]

Now that we know that the audience's WIIFM has to come first and be part of the framed key message so that relevance can be established, where does the credibility come in? When listeners are presented with a message, they try to determine whether the message is accurate and whether the source lacks credibility. (See Chapter Two for more information on credibility.)

The message's ability to have a persuasive impact is diminished when listeners attribute bias to a source. When credibility is low, the listener will discount the claims made in the message. Therefore, when a key message is framed, the listener is judging the credibility of the source.

Positively framed messages that are presented by those with perceived expertise will have the greatest influence on attitudes to the message.

Positively framed messages that are presented by those with perceived expertise will have the greatest influence on attitudes toward the message.

Like the frame, the WIIFM and key message, evidence of credibility must also come at the very start of your message.

Evidence exists suggesting that the message order, frame and credibility of the message source all influence the final judgment of the listener.[28]

▸ Application

The order and structure of your message really do matter. What I have learned through experience and research is that for effective persuasion, the order of your message should be as follows:

1. *Audience (What's In It For Me) – The audience must come first because everything is determined by relevance. The WIIFM must tie into the key message.*

2. *Credibility – Credibility must be the next step. It does not help to have it at the end. The listener needs it to determine its worth before he or she can listen to any of the details.*

3. *Order – Your framed WIIFM and credibility have to come right in the beginning of your message. Waiting until the end of the narrative structure is not effective for relevant persuasion.*

Argument, evidence, logic and data – once we have heard the elements above in the right order, we are now ready to hear the rest of the message.

Feel free to go to your worksheet and make sure that what you have done so far with Audience (WIIFM) and Credibility is in this persuasive structure, and check to make sure you have given your audience a clearly framed key message.

The persuasive structure does not always come easily since the narrative structure has been our dominant way to communicate throughout our lives.

If you have difficulty, write out your message in the way you typically do. Then take what you have written as your conclusion and put it as the first part of your message. This exercise will help get you used to the idea of getting to the point quickly.

Chapter Four: **R**emember me

In the last three chapters we examined how to start
your persuasive message. We discussed what impact the
relevance (WIIFM) of the **A**udience, **C**redibility, and
Order have on your message (the first three ingredients
to build our ACORN). If these elements are ignored,
the rest of the message will be much harder to listen to.

Now we are at the point in our message construction
where we convey the body of our message and the
facts of the argument to the listener that are sure to win
him or her over and make the listener **R**emember
our message.

In Chapter Two we talked briefly about Aristotle and
his keys to persuasion. We noted that logos is the
evidence, logic and argument. I find that in the seminars
I do for corporate clients, the argument is the part that
most people are good at. Once it is their turn to talk,
they have a lot of great information to share and usually
have solid arguments. Why then are they still not good
persuaders? Why does the audience still not listen
closely to their message?

Often, even though their data and argument are sound, when it is their turn to talk they want to tell their listeners EVERYTHING they know.

Often, even though their data and argument are sound, when it is their turn to talk they want to tell their listeners EVERYTHING they know. They want to flood listeners with ideas and facts and evidence. They do what is commonly referred to as a "data dump." It is like asking your listeners to take a sip of water from a fire hose.

The surge of data in our lives is well documented. Now that industrialized nations are shifting from an industrial society to a knowledge society, we live in an information economy.

Economics, however, is the study of how society uses scarce resources. One could argue that in our current society, information is not scarce. It is overflowing, and we are drowning in it. We are shifting to a new economy. A new fight is brewing over what might currently be the scarcest resource: our attention. We are now in an "attention economy."[29]

Many cognitive scientists are drawing a distinction between raw information and information we can use in thinking. They firmly believe that our listening problem is not information overload. They believe that the real problem is organization underload.

How can we help our listeners take a sip without drowning? How can we make sure to give our squirrel enough acorns without choking it?

There are three key factors that will influence how our messages are constructed and remembered:

1. Understanding how adults learn. How can we hear and make sense of what you are telling us?

2. Understanding memory. How much information can we hear and retain?

3. Getting the audience to take action.

Adult learning

There are many principles of adult learning that are now being recognized and implemented in training and education classes.

For persuasion, the most important element to understand is that adults simply learn differently than children.

For persuasion, the most important element to understand is that adults simply learn differently than children. Physiologically, when kids learn, they form cell assemblies and phase sequences. When kids learn, they are actually building these sequences. They are making new connections and forming them so that they can make sense of the world around them. (That is probably why when she was young, my daughter incessantly asked "Why?" after everything I said.)

As adults, we are not making new connections as we learn. We spend our time making new arrangements, connecting information to what we already know rather than learning "new" things. We constantly reinterpret our experiences and search to make meaning from them. This is how adults learn.[30]

In 1926, Piaget first introduced the term *schema*. Schema theory was developed in the 1970s. Schema theory views organized knowledge as a network of abstract structures. It is a mental framework that represents how we view the world. This schema changes as we encounter and learn new information. The interesting thing, however, is the realization that for adults, schemas are not built, but are only changed. There must be prior knowledge and experience forming the framework so that the newly formed information can attach.[31]

Why is this important? We are trying to provide new information to someone or want him or her to see something in a new way. Because of the way they learn, it is difficult for adults to understand new information without a lot of cognitive processing to figure out where this new information should fit into their existing schema.

As adults we would have to listen to the message, maintain our attention (which is not possible without relevance), then process the information, interpret the meaning, and then try to figure out where to attach it to the framework that already exists in our mind. That is a lot of work!

In a short conversation, how can we make this easier for the listener? Simple. Express your message in an easy-to-understand way that is completely accessible to the listener. If we can describe our message in terms that the listener already understands and can easily locate in his or her schema, our message will be more readily internalized. How do we do that? In a word: metaphor.

The use of metaphors, analogies and mnemonic devices can greatly assist the listener's initial understanding and more importantly the inclusion of this new information into his or her schema. This is especially true if you convey technical material for those listeners who do not have a background in that subject.

There is a great scene from the movie *My Cousin Vinny* that shows this brilliantly. Toward the end of the movie, the whole case of whether or not the two boys will be convicted of murder comes down to one last testimony. The witness finds the key piece of evidence and needs to convey this information to the jury, who all live in Alabama. She begins by describing a feature on some automobiles called "positraction."

The lawyer asks her to explain positraction so she can prove that the car the two boys were in could not have made the two equal-length tire marks leaving the crime scene and could not be the getaway car for the murder. She begins by defining positraction: "It's the limited slip differential which distributes power equally to both the right and left tires."

At this point in her testimony, the jury, which has no general automotive knowledge, is unimpressed by this evidence because they do not really understand its point. But then she goes on to say, "Which anyone who has been stuck in the mud in Alabama knows, you step on the gas, one tire spins, the other does nothing." After that sentence, the jury nods and completely understands.[32]

They understand her second sentence because they can easily grasp the idea and fit it into their schema of understanding. The first sentence requires technical knowledge the jury doesn't possess to connect to it, or a much more detailed explanation for them to find a way to understand this new information.

Metaphors and analogies are wonderful and powerful tools. They tell us new information that can be understood by our past experiences.

I saw the power of metaphors first hand when I was a sales trainer for an orthopedic company early in my career. We had produced a new surgical screwdriver with a special sleeve to hold onto the screw to help get it started into the hole. Removing the holding sleeve was not difficult to do, but it was difficult to explain because it had to be held with one hand and removed while holding the screwdriver in the other hand. In essence, you had to straddle your index and middle finger around the sleeve, and then use your thumb to depress the button to allow the sleeve to release, and then hold it down while you slide the sleeve along the axis of the screwdriver shaft.

That was hard to explain until one day as I was watching someone struggle with it, I blurted out, "Just hold it like a cigarette and push with your thumb and then slide it like a trombone." The understanding and response were immediate and correct. When I explained it the old way, they would get it, but it would take much longer for them to process. Even if they never had personal experience smoking a cigarette or playing a trombone, they had enough background knowledge to understand what it was like and quickly and easily embraced the analogy.

Memory

If you want your messages, your presentations (and you) to be more memorable, use simple language. In his 2007 book, *Words That Work*, Frank Luntz listed his ten rules of successful communication.[33] Rule number one and rule number two both deal with concise, simple language. Rule number one is to use small words, and rule number two is to use short sentences. Whenever we talk about this in my MBA communication classes at Wharton, the students push back and worry that they are "dumbing down" the message.

They may think they sound smarter by using big words and complex sentences, but if the listener doesn't easily and readily understand the message and cannot remember it, it will have no value.

A paper called "Consequences of Erudite Vernacular Utilized Irrespective of Necessity: Problems with Using Long Words Needlessly" was published in 2006. In this study 71 Stanford undergraduate students were asked to read passages of personal essays submitted as part of applications for graduate admissions. These passages were changed by the researchers to make them moderately complex or highly complex. For the highly complex passages, the researchers replaced every noun, verb and adjective with the longest possible thesaurus equivalent. For the moderately complex passages, the researchers made the same changes as above, but only to every third applicable word. The students were then asked to rate the passages.

They found that, "contrary to prevailing wisdom, increasing the complexity of a text does not cause an essay's author to seem more intelligent. In fact, the opposite appears to be true... Complexity neither disguised the shortcomings of poor essays, nor enhanced the appeal of high-quality essays." In the same article, the authors performed more experiments across disparate domains, different judgment types and different paradigms. The effects they found were the same. Basically, "...needless complexity leads to negative evaluations."[34]

"...needless complexity leads to negative evaluations."

Short, clear messages work best. Remember, it is not just about what you want to say, it is also about how best to get the audience to hear you.

Luntz draws our attention to our love of short messages that capture our attention, are easy to understand, and are easy to remember. He cites dozens of examples such as Nike's "Just Do It," 7Up's "The Un Cola" and Frosted Flakes', "They're Grrreat!" These short messages work because they are not only catchy, but completely and accurately summarize the meaning of those brands. You understand what 7Up is because of its slogan.

Mnemonics help us achieve the same thing. A mnemonic is a pattern of letters or idea associations that helps us remember something. You probably know some and consistently use them to help you remember. For example, you might remember the Great Lakes of the United States as HOMES—Huron, Ontario, Michigan, Erie, and Superior. You may remember the notes going up the lines on the treble clef are EGBDF or Every Good Boy Does Fine, or the notes on the spaces going up the treble clef as FACE. Hopefully you will remember a new one each time you want to recall the strategy to make your message more persuasive and maintain attention: ACORN—Audience, Credibility, Order of message, Remember me and Need to connect.

Although the concise 140-character limit of Twitter is so popular, and we love mnemonics, slogans, sound bites and headlines, your message can't be delivered in catchy phrases. However, as we discussed in the last chapter, your key message—the one idea you really want to get across—should be memorable and easy to understand. To achieve this it is helpful to think of your key message as a headline, slogan or sound bite.

Key messages need to be silver bullets, not buckshot from a shotgun. Don't throw everything you have at the listener. Instead, hone a shiny, pointed single message that will be short, easy to understand and memorable. The message points that can move into long-term memory will be the ones that differentiate your message from its competition.

How much can we hear and retain? — Chunking

After the key message, what can you do with the rest of your data? One of the biggest obstacles that my clients face is the ability to chunk information together and keep their evidence and data organized for the listener. If we are reading your message, you would probably put in headers, paragraph indentations, bullet points, bold or italic words, or even underline it to show your key points and message and to help the reader follow along through your logic.

Just because the message is spoken, doesn't mean that those needs of your audience have gone away. After giving a solid key message you need to carefully lead your listeners through your logic. A good way to do it is through thoughtful chunks of information.

As listeners, we just can't listen to many disparate pieces of information, quickly put them in order and fit them into our schema.

We need bite-size chunks of information so that we don't get overwhelmed.

We need bite-size chunks of information so that we don't get overwhelmed. As you create the body of your message, how can you organize the evidence and information to make it easier for us to get? Can you put the information together in chunks for us so that as listeners, we can skip that step?

We are not good at listening to a laundry list of information. In actuality, we can listen to no more than 3-5 ideas at a time. That is why no one thinks of their telephone number as a ten-digit number. They think of it in three chunks. 800-555-1212. Three is just plain easier than ten.

If a speaker got up in the front of a room and said, "Good morning, today I am going to go through the nineteen ways you can save money by clipping coupons," you would probably stop listening even if saving money fit your WIIFM (What's In It For Me). We just don't want to process that amount of data. That is why on the evening news, to keep our attention through that next commercial, newscasters tease us with just bite-size nuggets of information we can easily understand. For example, the anchor might say, "When we come back, three ways you can save your family money by clipping coupons." Even if the content is the same and there really are nineteen discrete ways to save that money, if they can put them into three chunks or categories, we will be more likely to want to listen.

Try this exercise; you may have seen others like it, but actually give this one a try. Time yourself and look at the list of symbols below for fifteen seconds.[35]

!@#$%#%@!$$#%@!@%!$##@%$!

At the end of the fifteen seconds, cover the list and write down as many as you remember in order.

_ _

Now, look at the next list for fifteen seconds.

!!!!!@@@@@#####$$$$$%%%%%

Now cover the list and write your answers down.

- -

If you are like most people, you had more right the second time even though each list has identical symbols (except for the order). If you think about it, this test is similar to an ideal listening environment. You found enough relevance to try the exercise. You are focused, and during the test your attention did not waiver (or at least not much in that fifteen seconds) and you knew that you were going to be immediately responsible for the information. If all our listeners had those things going for them, this message process would be a lot easier for us.

Let's talk about your process during the test. When you first looked at the first list, what did your mind try to do? The first thing it probably did was scan the entire list to look for a pattern. You most likely did not focus one by one on each symbol and try to memorize them in order. You wanted to find a pattern, a chunk, and an order.

This is a classic case of information entropy. Entropy is actually a thermodynamic quantity representing the amount of disorder or randomness in a system. Claude E. Shannon introduced the concept of information entropy or the randomness in content in his 1948 paper, "A Mathematical Theory of Communication."[36]

The first list has a high level of information entropy because the symbols are random. We cannot predict what comes next. As listeners, we want low information entropy. We want patterns. We want order. We cannot quickly and easily understand chaos.

We want patterns. We want order. We cannot quickly and easily understand chaos.

What was your reaction to the entropy? When I ask that question during my seminars, most of my participants say that they looked at the list once or twice, could not discern a pattern, and figured that in fifteen seconds they would never be able to remember it, so they gave up almost immediately. They did not see the missing pattern as a challenge to overcome. They did not work hard to achieve success. They just stopped trying. The same thing happens when your listeners cannot detect a pattern in your information. We will listen for a short bit, but if we can't predict what comes next, or see the order, we will be overwhelmed by the entropy of the message and stop listening.

Even though the content in the first list is identical to the content in the second list, when my participants see the second list, most let out a bit of a chuckle and when it is time, they put their pens to paper and get right to work. I have been asked whether there was some trick or if I cheated and gave them more time for the second list. They felt that the expired time was much more than fifteen seconds. The times were equal, but the presence of a structure helped them grasp and remember the information so easily that they didn't feel stressed or hurried.

How do you normally chunk your logic and data? Do you often just keep going down your list of facts without a preview to let the audience know what is coming? Is it just slide after slide and graph after graph that don't fit into themes or categories? Do you just blurt out all the benefits of the product from the marketing literature without caring about the listener?

Getting the audience to take action

Now that you have the beginning and middle of your message, how do you end? What should the conclusion be? We know it should no longer be the punch line or key message—we have shown that those items need to move to the beginning.

To figure out how to end, let's consider once more the definition of persuasion that we used in the introduction of this book. We defined persuade as "to move by argument, entreaty, or expostulation to a belief, position, or course of action." Now that we have given our listeners our message, we need to ask them to take the action.

There is nothing worse than actually being persuaded but then walking out of the room and losing that feeling of wanting to change or to help or to act. Therefore, the final part of the message must be a clear and concise call to action.

In the 1930's a scholar from Purdue University named Alan H. Monroe created a sequence of steps based on the psychology of persuasion that he hoped would inspire people to take action. Two of the steps in his sequence I find necessary when trying to persuade. One is the action step, and the other is visualization, which we will talk about in the next chapter.[37]

In the persuasive structure we are talking about, as well as Monroe's structure, the action step serves as the concluding step. Now that the audience has heard your message, and perhaps a summary of your message if it was long or complex, the audience needs to know what to do.

When you provide your listeners your call to action, there are three things to remember:

1. When you tell your listeners what to do, be as specific as possible. Should they vote, try the product, write to their congressman? Exactly what should they do?

2. Make sure that what you ask them to do is doable. Don't ask for too much money or even an all-out commitment. Is there an easy way for them to do what you want, or at least to start to do it?

3. Make sure the call to action is something they can do very soon after you ask. If there is too much time between asking and doing, the listeners will lose their passion for the idea and forget.[38]

There are many things you can do to help your listeners not only remember the message (and you) but also distinguish your messages from the competition:

- Understand how adults learn and pay attention to message complexity.

- Use metaphors or mnemonics so that you can more easily fit new information into their schema.

- Speak in short, clear (catchy, if possible) phrases, especially for your key message.

- Chunk the information so that the listener can easily see order and predict what is next.

- Specifically direct the listener on what to do next.

▸ Application

Remember the TV guy from Chapter One? When we last talked about him, he had kept in mind the Audience (wife's WIIFM), took time to show his Credibility (TV research), had Organized his elements (key message first), and was ready to give her the details of his plan in a way that would allow her to understand and Remember his message.

He had found his wife's WIIFM: gaining the ability to entertain and have parties in their home.

His framed key message was, "Honey, I know how much you used to love it when your parents hosted parties and entertained their friends. You know, maybe we should really start to do more of that. Now that the holidays are over, why don't we plan a fun party for the Super Bowl or St. Patrick's Day? We can decorate the house, finally get a nice new TV and share some special time with our friends and family."

For credibility, he said, "To make sure we get the best quality TV for the best value while staying in our budget, I have done lots of research. I started out by going to Consumer Reports *to find the best objectively rated brand, looked at online reviews to see what others like us think of their quality and value, and then looked at all of the Sunday circulars to find the best price."*

Now he is ready to tell her all the details and provide examples using concise wording and metaphors or examples she will understand. He chose three main chunks to help us follow his points.

Fits well in our plans to entertain

Best TV

Best price

Keep in mind that he will pick only the evidence that would support his key message of enhancing the ability to entertain. Keeping the key message or main point in mind will help filter which information to give and what might be more relevant to say at another time.

For example, he may want to keep the technical details of his decision of plasma vs LCD for a later discussion or in case she has questions. He wants to focus his evidence on features that will help when entertaining. He may want to explain why it is important to buy a TV that allows you to view from an oblique angle so that every guest can have a good view.

Lastly, he will pose to her his specific call to action, which may be to go shopping with him this weekend since they are having a big sale.

Now it's your turn again. Check that so far you have a solid WIIFM and framed key message, that you included credibility, and that you have everything in the best order. Now build in your facts and evidence, paying careful consideration to using clear and concise evidence that supports your key message. Use metaphors or mnemonics to facilitate understanding. Make sure you have no more than five chunks. It is your job to overcome information entropy. And lastly, have a specific call to action.

Chapter Five: **N**eed to connect

So far we have seen the need to think first and foremost about how our message will be relevant to our **A**udience, and we have seen the need to show our **C**redibility early in the message. We learned the proven impact the **O**rder of your message will have in persuasion as well as some tools to make the body of your message easy to listen to, stay engaged with and **R**emember (ACOR of our ACORN Communication Strategy™).

Now we are ready for the final tool to get your audience (squirrel) to listen (focus): the **N**eed for emotional connection to the message.

In Chapter Two we briefly talked about Aristotle and his three elements of persuasion that have withstood the test of time. In that chapter we discussed ethos or credibility. In Chapter Four we talked about logos or logical argument. The third element that Aristotle found as an essential element of persuasion is pathos or emotion.

This is the point in every MBA class I teach when the students roll their eyes at me. They inform me that they are business and finance people and that they deal in facts and figures, not fluffy bunnies and pretty butterflies. They are not sure they buy the emotional IQ argument that has persisted through the decades. Perhaps their reluctance comes from a fundamental misunderstanding of what Aristotle meant by emotion.

True, not all topics lend themselves to great expressions of emotion. But, as Aristotle suggested, there must be a balance between the objective nature of logos and the subjective nature of pathos. If you are raising money for breast cancer awareness, more pathos may be required in inspiring women who are survivors of this terrible disease. If you are pitching stocks to a business audience, more logos may be needed. It all depends on the topic and the audience. But regardless of what you say to whom, there must always be a balance.

We see in the very definition of persuasion that we must be MOVED toward our new belief or action. We cannot be moved if we don't feel anything for the subject.

As Jim Rohn said, "Effective communication is 20% what you know and 80% how you feel about what you know.[39] "Or as Dale Carnegie said, "When dealing with people, remember you are not dealing with creatures of logic, but creatures of emotion."[40]

Why is this true? Why are emotions so important? Are they really part of everything, even for people who are not generally emotionally demonstrative?

The answer is yes. There is a part of the brain called the *amygdala* (ə-mĭg'də-lə). This is the emotional part of the brain. The amygdala allows for empathy and feelings of emotion. Interestingly, it also controls the fight or flight reflex.

Even though we don't consciously know it, when the amygdala perceives something, it can bias us and cause us to think or act a certain way.[41] When the amygdala is triggered, a rush of hormones is activated and floods the body before the prefrontal lobes (the thinking part of the brain that regulates executive function) can mediate the reaction.[42]

Although we may not still need the "eat or be eaten" survival instinct while listening (hopefully), the brain cannot differentiate a physical threat from a threat to our ego. We just react.[43] When the amygdala acts and overrides our rational thought, it is known as the amygdala hijack. Basically, evolution has made humans emotional animals.

Basically, evolution has made humans emotional animals.

A recent well-known example of the amygdala hijack happened in Washington, D.C., on September 9, 2009, during a speech President Barack Obama was making to Congress. The President was commenting on his reform strategy when the shout of "You lie!" came from Representative Joe Wilson, R-S.C.

Joe Wilson could not control his amygdala. His thinking brain did not have a chance to catch up to the emotion. Even though he believed what he said and would have liked to make a rational comment on the situation, he was emotionally hijacked.

After his outburst, he drew immediate condemnation from both political parties. In his written statement of apology he said, "This evening I let my emotions get the best of me when listening to the President's remarks regarding the coverage of illegal immigrants in the health care bill. While I disagree with the president's statement, my comments were inappropriate and regrettable. I extend sincere apologies to the president for this lack of civility."[44]

Effective communicators are not necessarily looking to drive their audience toward emotional outbursts, but they need to get them to feel something about their message.

In addition to always being present, researchers have also suggested that emotion and feeling are related to perceiving and processing information, reasoning, memory retrieval, memory storage and learning.[45] The fact is that emotional material is processed more deeply than nonemotional material.[46]

This is why we often remember events and times that cause us to have strong feelings (grief, frustration, anger, embarrassment) more specifically than events that did not trigger such an emotional response.

For us to be effective communicators emotion must be part of every message. We must find a way to connect to the audience if we want to move them toward a new belief or action. If we fail to engage them emotionally, we will fail to persuade.

The question then becomes: how can you work emotion into your messages without getting too fluffy or dramatic? Simple: it is just a matter of word choice.

As they say, a picture is worth a thousand words and if the audience can see it or visualize it, then they can feel it. Here are three good ways to get emotion into your message to help the audience visualize the outcome.

1. Use word choice to promote connotation.

2. Use vivid language in word choice to help tell a detailed story and visualize the outcome.

3. Use word choice to make the abstract something we can understand within the intended context.

Connotation

Word choice is a fairly easy way to marry logos to pathos. Many words have strong connotations. Words that have heavy connotations cannot only communicate meaning, but convey emotion as well. Compare the words on the next page. Even though they are similar, do you respond more to the words on the right? Do they evoke a visceral connection from you? Do you think their use would make you care more about the topic or data to which they are ascribed?

Taste	Savor
Dislike	Hate
Inexpensive	Cheap
Situation	Crisis
Spread	Epidemic
Large	Colossal
Big	Enormous
Hard	Challenging
Fly	Soar
Needed	Urgent
Quality	Luxury
Interesting	Fascinating
Rare	Endangered
Honest	Genuine
Tight	Crammed
Smart	Shrewd
Better	Improved
Worry	Panic

Visualization

Word choice can also help us visualize. In the last chapter we talked about Alan Monroe and his motivating sequence that has influenced how we think about persuasion. He believed that to persuade your listeners, you need to use vivid language and details to help them either see the positive relief that your solution would bring or, perhaps sometimes more powerfully, show the horrible outcome if your solution is not adopted. This is called the visualization step.

These images will cause us to have an emotional response. These images carry not only fact, but implicit meaning as well. We will see the fact in the context of the meaning provided by the connotation.

For example, think of something as short but as powerful as the most well-known part of the inscription on the base of the Statue of Liberty:

> Cries she with silent lips, "Give me your tired, your poor, your huddled masses yearning to breathe free. The wretched refuse of your teeming shore. Send these, the homeless, tempest-tossed to me. I lift my lamp beside the golden door."

This was a sonnet written in 1883 by poet Emma Lazarus entitled "The New Colossus."[47] Lazarus could have written, "All are welcome," but she chose more vivid language to help us better understand, connect to and feel the plight of immigrants making the journey across the ocean.

Now, most of you are probably not as poetic as Emma Lazarus, or as talented with word choice, but even picking one or two vivid words that help the audience visualize your message or make a story from your facts will help them fulfill the need for pathos that they have.

Of course, your entire message should not be one long story, but the words around your key messages should be one. If you make your whole message a story, it will gain emotion, but will lose the benefits of message order described in Chapter Three.

Making abstract concrete

The benefit of good word choice is not only in helping us understand and feel your key points, but also in helping us make better sense of and connect better with numbers and statistics.

For example, in 1988, famous talk show host Oprah Winfrey lost a total of sixty-seven pounds. Sure, that sounds impressive, but we really can't visualize what sixty-seven pounds of fat is. If she had just announced on the air that she had lost sixty-seven pounds, we probably would have soon forgotten her message.

But instead of saying she lost sixty-seven pounds, she actually wheeled a wagon full of sixty-seven pounds of fat onto the stage. Because of that stark visualization, no one could forget that image.

We understood her weight loss and connected to her message. Regrettably for Oprah, she regained that weight and because we could never forget that image, it was news again, years later.

Our goal is to make the abstractness of numbers and statistics more concrete. We need to make the numbers meaningful and understandable so that we can connect and feel something about them. For example, which statement do you feel is most powerful?

The disease spread through the United States and affected 56,886 people.

Or

The disease became an epidemic that swept through the United States, infecting enough people to fill New York Yankee Stadium to capacity.

Letting us see and understand the context of the numbers helps us connect.

I once heard an old Irish saying (although I am not really sure it is Irish) that seems to summarize the content of this chapter. It goes like this: "You may forget what I told you, you may forget what I showed you, but you will never forget how I made you feel."

▸ Application

Once again, it is your turn. Feel free to go to your worksheet and complete this last part of the exercise. What words can be chosen to help make your point and message? Once you have a few, use them in wording your key messages. Use any opportunity you have to make abstract facts and numbers more concrete. I have found that in my seminars, for this part of the exercise, it is often helpful to have someone to bounce ideas off of. Sometimes this more creative part of messaging works well in a brainstorming format.

I hope you have found your journey through this exercise and this book to be practical, helpful and mind-changing. I hope I have moved you toward a new belief and inspired you to act.

The acorn is what gets a squirrel to focus. Without this focus, it could not take in what it needs.

Your listeners need to focus on your message so that they can hear, understand and remember you, and so that you can give them what they need.

If you just take a few minutes before your next high-stake conversation to review the ACORN Communication Strategy™ and apply its easy principles, your next message will be more persuasive and yield better results.

The recipe is easy to understand and apply.

Audience – Find their relevance and WIIFM.

Credibility – Tell them through your personal or credentialed credibility why you are the right person to help solve the problem

Order of Message – Use the persuasive structure with your framed key message first.

Remember – Make your data and evidence easy for adults to hear by chunking and using easy-to-remember language, metaphors and mnemonics. Give them a strong call to action.

Need to Connect – Use word choice to move your audience toward engagement with your message.

When you have done all these things your message will be ready. Now go nuts!

Chapter Six: What now

Communication is a skill that you can learn. It's like riding a bicycle or typing. If you're willing to work at it, you can rapidly improve the quality of every part of your life.

Brian Tracy[48]

It would be wonderful if all we needed to do was read a book on communication to be masterful at it. Even though the concepts in this book are easy to understand and apply to your everyday life, there may be high-stakes circumstances when you require some guided practice.

Here are some helpful resources:

Personal resources

Visit: www.uhmms.com for more details

Online virtual coaching

Finally, an interactive on-line experience with targeted personal feedback.

Simply upload your video and get a professional critique to help transform your ability to get a message across.

Public seminars

One-day seminars on the ACORN Communication Strategy™ open to the public.

Resource portal

Sign up on the website for access to the resource portal, which provides tips, articles, Mp3 downloads and interviews.

Corporate resources

Visit: www.uhmms.com for more details

Speaker services

Author Dr. Patricia Scott provides keynote presentations as well as corporate training events based on the ACORN Communication Strategy™.

Bulk book purchase

Uhmms offers excellent discounts on this book when ordered in quantity for bulk purchase or special sales. For more information, please contact Uhmms.

Chapter Seven: Tools

Over the next few pages, there are some tools to help you polish your ACORN. The first tool is a copy of the worksheet we have been using throughout the book to create your message. I have also included a list of several other books that are particularly helpful in developing a persuasive mindset. I hope you found this book to be practical, easy to understand and even easier to implement. Enjoy watching your squirrels eat.

ACORN Communication Strategy™ Worksheet

Situation:

_____

_____

_____

Five Elements of Persuasion

1. Audience "What's In It For Me?"

_____

_____

2. Credibility

_____

_____

3. Order of message

_____

_____

4. Remember

_____

_____

5. Need to connect

_____

_____

Recommended Persuasion Reading List

Cialdini, R.B. (2007) *Influence: The Psychology of Persuasion.* New York: William Morrow and Company, Inc.

Duarte, N. (2008) *Slide:ology: The Art and Science of Creating Great Presentations.* Sebastopol, CA: O'Reilly Media.

Goldstein, N.J., Martin, S.J., Cialdini, R.B. (2008) *Yes: 50 Scientifically Proven Ways to Be Persuasive.* New York: Free Press.

Heath, C., Heath, D. (2008) *Made to Stick: Why Some Ideas Survive and Others Die.* New York: Random House.

Magnacca, M. (2009) *So What?: How to Communicate What Really Matters to Your Audience.* Upper Saddle River, NJ: FT Press.

Maxwell, R., Dickman, R. (2007) *The Elements of Persuasion: Using Storytelling to Pitch Better, Sell Faster and Win More Business.* New York: HarperCollins.

Miller, A. (2004) *Metaphorically Selling.* New York: Chiron Associates, Inc.

Morgan, N.H. (2003) *Working the Room: How to Move People to Action through Audience-Centered Speaking.* Boston, MA: Harvard Business School Publishing.

Simmons, A., Lipman, D. (2006) *The Story Factor.* Cambridge, MA: Basic Books.

Notes

1. *WikiAnswers—What is the attention span of a squirrel.* (n.d.).
    Retrieved April 14, 2010, from http://wiki.answers.
    com/Q/What_is_the_attention_span_of_a_squirrel

2. BBC News | SCI/TECH | Turning into digital goldfish.
    (n.d.). *BBC NEWS | News Front Page.* Retrieved
    November 06, 2009, from http://news.bbc.co.uk/2/hi/
    science/nature/1834682.stm

3. Guiniven, J. (2008). Keeping the op-ed effective in today's
    media climate. *Public Relation Tactics*, 15(10), 6.

4. Dieken, C. (2009). *Talk Less, Say More: Three Habits to
    Influence Others and Make Things Happen.* Hoboken, NJ:
    John Wiley & Sons.

5. Tucker, P. (2009). The Dawn of the Postliterate Age. *The
    Futurist* (Nov-Dec), 41-45.

6. Postman, N. (1986). *Amusing Ourselves to Death: Public
    Discourse in the Age of Show Business.* New York: Penguin
    Books.

7. de Moraes, L.—Obama's State of the Union won't preempt
    season premiere of 'Lost' after all - washingtonpost.com.
    (n.d.). *Washingtonpost.com - nation, world, technology and
    Washington area news and headlines.* Retrieved January
    27, 2010, from http://www.washingtonpost.com/wpdyn/
    content/article/2010/01/08/AR2010010803616.html

8. Erma Bombeck Quotes : Quoteland : *Quotations by Author.
    (n.d.). Quoteland.com - Quotations on every topic, by every
    author, and in every fashion possible.* Retrieved February
    19, 2010, from http://www.quoteland.com/author.
    asp?AUTHOR_ID=1275

9. Persuade—Definition and More from the Merriam-Webster Dictionary. (n.d.). *Dictionary and Thesaurus - Merriam-Webster Online*. Retrieved January 25, 2010, from http://www.merriam-webster.com/dictionary/persuade

10. A Squirrel Place F.A.Q. Section. (n.d.). *The All New Squirrel Place*. Retrieved February 10, 2010, from http://www.squirrels.org/faq.html

11. Dale Carnegie Quotes. (n.d.). *Famous Quotes and Quotations at BrainyQuote*. Retrieved February 19, 2010, from http://www.brainyquote.com/quotes/quotes/d/dalecarneg156624.html

12. Aristotle. (1991). *Aristotle on rhetoric: a theory of civic discourse* (G. A. Kennedy, Trans.). New York: Oxford University Press.

13. Shell, G. R., & Moussa, M. (2007). *The art of woo: using strategic persuasion to sell your ideas*. New York: Portfolio.

14. Sincerity. (n.d.). *Wikipedia, the free encyclopedia*. Retrieved February 09, 2010, from http://en.wikipedia.org/wiki/Sincerity

15. *AIG Executives Blow $440,000 After Getting Bailout - FOXBusiness.com*. (n.d.). Retrieved April 14, 2010, from http://www.foxbusiness.com/story/markets/industries/finance/aig-executives-blow--getting-bailout/

16. *AIG Cancels Another Resort Meeting After Criticism* (Update1). (n.d.). *Bloomberg.com*. Retrieved April 05, 2010, from http://www.bloomberg.com/apps/news?sid=ajC0ofGADFu0&pid=20601103

17. Allgeier, S. (2009, June). Personal Credibility Is the New PC. *Training and Development*, 76-77.

18. Elsasser, J. (2009, October). Study: Credibility of News Media Hits Two Decade Low. *Tactics*.

19. Tucker, P. (2009). The Dawn of the Postliterate Age. *The Futurist* (Nov-Dec), 41-45.

20. Sweetser, K. D., Porter, L. V., Chung, D. S., & Kim, E. (2008). Credibility and the Use of Blogs Among Professionals in the Communication Industry. *Journalism & Mass Communication Quarterly,* 85(1), 169-185.

21. Conger, J. A. (1998). The Necessary Art of Persuasion. *Harvard Business Review,* May-June, 84-95.

22. Buda, R., & Zhang, Y. (2000). Consumer product evaluation: the interactive effect of message framing, presentation order, and source credibility. *Journal of Product and Brand Management,* 9(4), 229-242.

23. Fairhurst, G. T. (1996). The *art of framing: managing the language of leadership.* San Francisco: Jossey-Bass.

24. Sussman, L. (1999). How to Frame a Message: The Art of Persuasion and Negotiation. *Business Horizons,* 117-121.

25. Buda, R., & Zhang, Y. (2000). Consumer product evaluation: the interactive effect of message framing, presentation order, and source credibility. *Journal of Product and Brand Management,* 9(4), 229-242.

26. Haugtvedt, C. P., & Wegener, D. T. (1994). Message Order Effects in Persuasion: An Attitude Strength Perspective. *Journal of Consumer Research,* 21, 205-218.

27. Baker, W. E., Honea, H., & Russell, C. A. (2004). Do Not Wait to Reveal the Brand Name. *Journal of Advertising,* 33(3), 77-85.

28. Buda, R., & Zhang, Y. (2000). Consumer product evaluation: the interactive effect of message framing, presentation order, and source credibility. *Journal of Product and Brand Management,* 9(4), 229-242.

29. Attention Shoppers. (n.d.). *Wired News.* Retrieved February 23, 2010, from http://www.wired.com/wired/archive/5.12/es_attention.html

30. How Adults Learn :: Ageless Learner. (n.d.). *Ageless Learner :: Curious for Life!* Retrieved February 24, 2010, from http://agelesslearner.com/intros/adultlearning.html

31. Schema theory of learning. (n.d.). *SIL International: Partners in Language Development.* Retrieved February 24, 2010, from http://www.sil.org/lingualinks/literacy/ImplementALiteracyProgram/SchemaTheoryOfLearning.htm

32. Lynn, J. (Director). (1992). *My Cousin Vinny* [Motion picture on DVD]. 20th Century Fox.

33. Luntz, F. (2007). *Words that work: it's not what you say, it's what people hear.* New York: Hyperion.

34. Oppenheimer, D. M. (2006). Consequences of Erudite Vernacular Utilized Irrespective of Necessity: Problems with Using Long Words Needlessly. *Applied Cognitive Psychology, 20,* 139-156.

35. Adapted from Stolovitch, H. D., & Keeps, E. J. (2002). *Telling ain't training* (pp. 63-64). Alexandria, VA: ASTD.

36. Shannon, C. E. (1948). A mathematical theory of communication. *Bell System Technical Journal, 27,* 379-423, 623-656.

37. Monroe's motivated sequence. (n.d.). *Wikipedia, the free encyclopedia.* Retrieved February 25, 2010, from http://en.wikipedia.org/wiki/Monroe's_motivated_sequence

38. Persuasion: Monroe's Motivated Sequence. (n.d.). *Free Articles Directory | Submit Articles—ArticlesBase.com.* Retrieved February 25, 2010, from http://www.articlesbase.com/public-speaking-articles/persuasion-monroes-motivated-sequence-989543.html

39. Jim Rohn Quotes : Quoteland : Quotations by Author. (n.d.). *Quoteland.com—Quotations on every topic, by every author, and in every fashion possible.* Retrieved February 25, 2010, from http://www.quoteland.com/author.asp?AUTHOR_ ID=2030

40. Dale Carnegie Quotes. (n.d.). *Famous Quotes and Quotations at BrainyQuote.* Retrieved February 25, 2010, from http://www.brainyquote.com/quotes/quotes/d/ dalecarneg130727.html

41. Adolphs, R. (2009). The Social Brain: Neural Basis of Social Knowledge. *The Annual Review of Psychology,* 60, 693-716.

42. What Was I Thinking? Handling the Hijack—Human Capital—Business Management US | GDS Publishing. (n.d.). *International Business Management News | GDS Publishing.* Retrieved February 25, 2010, from http:// www.busmanagement.com/article/What-Was-I-Thinking-Handling-the-Hijack/

43. FOXNews.com—Congressman Yells 'You Lie' at Obama During Speech. (n.d.). Breaking News | Latest News | Current News - FOXNews.com. Retrieved March 2, 2010, from http://www.foxnews.com/ politics/2009/09/10/congressman-yells-lie-obama-speech/

44. *Outsmart Your Brain.* (n.d.). Retrieved February 26, 2010, from http://www.outsmartyourbrain.com

45. Dirkx, J. M. (2001). The Power of Feelings: Emotion, Imagination, and the Construction of Meaning in Adult Learning. *New Directions for Adult and Continuing Education,* 89, 63-72.

46. Carstensen, L. L., & Turk-Charles, S. (1994). The Salience of Emotion Across the Adult Life Span. *Psychology and Aging,* 9(2), 259-264.

47. *The Statue of Liberty—History and Key Facts*. (n.d.). Retrieved April 14, 2010, from http://manhattan.about.com/od/historyandlandmarks/a/statueofliberty.htm

48. Brian Tracy Quotes : Quoteland : Quotations by Author. (n.d.). *Quoteland.com—Quotations on every topic, by every author, and in every fashion possible*. Retrieved February 19, 2010, from http://www.quoteland.com/author.asp?AUTHOR_ID=8331

Acknowledgments

I am the luckiest woman in the world.

As a young girl I had a mother who showed me the value of hard work, taught me that nothing would be handed to me because it must be earned, and showed me the value of an education.

As an adult, I have a wonderful family, as well as caring friends and colleagues who all generously, and without hesitation, told me that they would be happy to try to help make this book a success.

My husband Dan and daughter Emily endured and even enjoyed countless hours in the car and over family meals talking about the concepts of the book, debating wording and helping find a great picture of a squirrel. And perhaps, even more impressively, they became ruthless evangelists for the book and its concepts. My then 6-year-old daughter would easily recite, without notes, the five key points of the ACORN Communication Strategy™ to anyone willing to listen.

I apologize to my extended family (cousins, in-laws, aunts and uncles) who when at a family gathering would merely say, "what's new?" and have to listen to our enthusiasm for this project for hours.

I am also fortunate to work with a truly gifted and passionate group of colleagues in the Communication Program at The Wharton School at the University of Pennsylvania. These talented professionals endlessly strive to make each student a leader. They don't just teach; they constantly work on crafting an environment where each student not only understands but also internalizes the art and science of communication. Margaret Lambires and Carl Maugeri, Senior Associate Directors of the Wharton Communication Program, have been generously sharing their time and their knowledge with me over the past several years. Without their inspiration, this strategy would have never been conceived.

I owe a debt of gratitude to Susan Little, Heidi Hausner, Paula Rutledge, Kelly McBride, Lisa Sheldon, Linda Garrett, Cory Carter, Ted Ledeboer and Tina Genest who painstakingly went the extra mile to read, correct and comment on the early drafts of this work.

Lastly, I want to thank and acknowledge the professionals who actually made this a real book: Steve Harrison and Debra Englander helped me get my message across. David Laughlin who designed the book and cover and Sheila Fuentes and Janice Fisher who edited the book.

Breinigsville, PA USA
27 December 2010
252108BV00001B/3/P